Adv **Book**

Having liv   than 2 decades, going through *5Cs of Mother India* brought back many memories and enhanced my love for our mother India. Sharvesh is so talented and I really liked the intent behind each C, style, type, and simplicity in crafting it.

Dr. Vidhya Vinod
CEO, Study World Education Holding Ltd.
Dubai International Academic City

It is indeed astonishing that at the age of 14, Sharvesh has written 50 poems in just 30 days! Through these poems, Sharvesh has brought out the greatness of Indian culture and has brilliantly depicted some of the great personalities influenced by this great culture. I sincerely invoke the Grace of the Lord and the blessings of Pujya Gurudev for his efforts.

With sincere prayers
Swami Aparajitananda, Chinmaya Mission

5Cs of Mother India explained by Gen Z of India! I could see Sharvesh's 'curiosity' in knowing the 'culture' of our India, his 'compassion' in explaining the Cs with great 'courage'. To conclude, let us all 'celebrate' him for the success of this beautiful attempt.

Dr.R. Gopalakrishnan
Principal K.S.Rangasamy College of Technology,
Tiruchengode

Advance praise for the book continued...

5 very diverse Cs, and Sharvesh has managed to integrate them flawlessly. This book promises lucid phrases mixed with traditional ideas making it a wholesome and excellent read. This was a journey that I didn't want to end.

Chitra Ananthakrishnan

Sharvesh has ingested and beautifully composed verses on key Indian leaders and their qualities, popular festivals, architectural marvels, and everything that is extraordinary about India, which is all very refreshing and enjoyable. Wish you further success and look forward to more of your publications!

Ramya Ragupathy
Head - Data Analytics,
Humanitarian OpenStreetMap Team

This book is a beautiful representation of our Supreme *Bharata Mata* and her rich heritage. It projects the immense cultural knowledge and pride imparted by Sharvesh's parents resulting in this marvellous collection of poems through judicious use of his precious time. All the best boy! I am proud of you! Every child and youth of India must read this and be proud of our heritage. *Om Bharata Gauravaaya Namaha!*

Vinod Viswanathan
Chinmaya Yuva Kendra

Your talent determines what you can do while your motivation determines how much you are willing to do. Your attitude determines how well you do it! Sharvesh is bestowed with exceptional talent, extraordinary motivation, and a winning attitude. He is a success in whatever he does. When I initially read his work, I was stupefied looking at the flair of his language. In his debut publication, *Treasured droplets*, I knew that the literary world was starting to get a glimpse of his talent yet to come. His writings were inquisitive, soothing to read and thought-provoking all at once. I was not surprised to learn that his second manuscript was now ready! Because he is Sharvesh, he can and will do it. In *5Cs of Mother India*, he touches upon interesting topics like Celebrations, Culture, Curiosity, Compassion, and Courage. Each of these bring forth so much emotion and memories associated with them, and Sharvesh has done a wonderful job penning down his feelings pertaining to each. May you keep writing and blossom in the literary world!

Gaanappriya Mohan Yogesh
Author & Scientist

The 5Cs of Mother India

Celebrating India in all its Glory

An Anthology of Poems by

P. G. Sharvesh

First Edition, 2022

Copyright © P G Sharvesh, 2022

All rights reserved. No part of this publication may be reproduced, distributed, or transmitted in any form or by any means, including photocopying, recording, or other electronic or mechanical methods, without the prior written permission of the author, except in the case of brief quotations embodied in critical reviews and certain other non-commercial uses permitted by copyright law. For permission requests, write to the publisher.

This book can be exported from India only by the publishers or by the authorized suppliers. Infringement of this condition of sale will lead to Civil and Criminal prosecution.

Paperback ISBN: 978-81-976876-3-1
eBook ISBN: 978-93-90508-50-1

Note: Due care and diligence has been taken while editing and printing the book; neither the author nor the publishers of the book hold any responsibility for any mistake that may have inadvertently crept in.

The publishers shall not be liable for any direct, consequential, or incidental damages arising out of the use of the book. In case of binding mistakes, misprints, missing pages, etc., the publishers' entire liability, and your exclusive remedy, is replacement of the book within one month of purchase by similar edition/reprint of the book.

Published by DIGITAL SPINES.
Originally published by 16Leaves.

Printed and bound in India.

Acknowledgment

I would like to thank the Lord Almighty for giving me such wonderful parents who have constantly supported and encouraged me to write poems and stories. I am also grateful for their guidance through their extensive vocabulary.

I send my best regards to the publisher, Bharath Parthasarathy, who voluntarily agreed to produce and popularize my book.

My humble Pranams to my Gurus and mentors for their motivation and blessings.

Contents

Curiosity

Courage

Compassion

Preface

Beauty lies in the eyes of the beholder and in the following pages is a selection of poems from Sharvesh's view of India. It is impossible to capture the rich culture and heritage of this country, right from Kashmir to Kanyakumari, within the span of a few pages. *The 5Cs of Mother India* is a small attempt to showcase the Celebrations, Culture, Curiosity, Courage, and Compassion through heart-felt poems to reminisce. Each section has 10 poems portraying architecture, history, technology, legends, trends, science, value systems and much more that India has to offer.

How this anthology came to be

On turning 14, Sharvesh published his first ever book on poetry. The encouragement that he received from his parents prompted him to attempt this poetical representation of glorious India's rich culture and heritage.

With his mother mentoring him, Sharvesh spent the lockdown of the 2020 pandemic in a constructive manner, penning down 2 poems each day and 3 on the weekends, all along diligently attending online school classes. The idea behind the one-month deadline was inspired by Honourable prime minister Narendra Modi's Mentoring Yuva scheme. Halfway through, Sharvesh learnt that poetry was not an accepted genre, and without a blink he shelved this book and wrote a science fiction with equal passion.

But the idea of interpreting India through poetry had set in his mind and in July the same year he returned to this manuscript. Sharvesh challenged himself again with a one-month deadline, and this quaint anthology of poems that you hold was the result of the challenge.

Not wanting to limit this interpretation to just his own views, he informally conducted a survey amongst a diverse set of profiles and cultures across the nation using the below questions:

- **Celebrations**: What would be the top 3 celebrations in your state according? And why?
- **Culture:** What is unique about your state, tradition or culture that is good to learn and spread the word about?
- **Curiosity:** When we talk about innovations and inventions, who comes to your mind, and for what reason?
- **Courage**: Who was the symbol of courage in history?
- **Compassion**: Who/what would you think of when you talk about compassion?

The answers to the survey became the framework for this book and prompted him to pen down his thoughts. It has been an enlightening and heart-warming journey to witness this book take shape. We hope you derive as much joy from it.

Celebrations

Image credit: cleanpng.com

Makar Sankranti, also known as Uttarayan, Pongal, Maghi or Poush Sankranti, is a harvest festival expressing the joy of common man at the bounty of crops as a blessing from Mother Earth.

Makar Sankranti

Time of the Uttarayan,
Celebrated on 14th Jan,
Dedicated to honouring the Sun,
Marks when the Sun passes through star Capricorn.
In Rajasthan, there is the Kumbh Mela,
People bathe in the Prayaga.
A confluence of Ganga and Yamuna,
That was started by Adi Shankaracarya.
In Assam, it is Magh Bihu,
Pongal in the state Tamil Nadu.
Makar Sankranti in Karnataka,
And Sankranti in Telangana.
First day in Bhogi Pongal,
Second is Thai Pongal,
In third place comes Mattu Pongal,
And at last, there is the Kaanum Pongal.
States and countries have different functions,
There are constant variations.
A multi-day harvest festival,
To thank Sun God and cattle,
For the plentiful harvest.

Image credit: clipart-library.com

Holi, celebrated through spraying of colours on each other, strengthens the social and secular fabric of India, marking the triumph of good over evil.

Holi

Holi is the festival of colours & love,
Where everything is lush.
Colours are thrown everywhere,
But in the heart, it's always there.

Holi marks the day of spring,
Which is the start of every good happening.
Celebrated in many places,
Always colour rushes,
The day when innate evil is destroyed,
And everyone is overjoyed.

Each throw colour powder,
And cause a bit of litter,
Our happy faces glitter.

We all will be content,
And to God, we will be better servants.

All of us eat and drink,
Keep enjoying till the brink.
Holi is great,
Our compassion rises innate.

Ramadan

Festival of fasting, reflecting and community,
Lasts for days 29 to 30,
Predawn meal of Suhur,
Fast till dusk to rediscover,
Feast breaking the fast is Iftar,
Fruits, Porridge, Samosa & Sweets,
The best way to break the fast at Masjid.
People should do their prayer,
And refrain from any sinful behaviour.
The word Ramadan means scorching hot,
People fasted to prevent a drought.
Muslims donate a large portion of zaket,
During this Ramadan month.
Many recite the entire Quran,
Some recite one juz each of 30 tarawih sessions,
Covering five times a day with devotion,
A time to cleanse soul,
And not to do things foul.

Image credit: freepik.com

Rakshabandhan is the bond of safety between a brother and a sister where sisters pray for the long life of brothers and brothers vow to keep their sisters away from harm.

Raksha Bandhan

Observed in the last day of the month Shravana,
Celebrated in various places across South Asia.
Sisters tie a Rakhi,
On their brother's hand symbolising responsibility,
And a beacon of Unity,
That enables us to live our life with harmony,
Brahmans change their sacred thread on this day,
Understanding sisters who care fondly.
Everyone celebrates Rakhi,
Including those in the National assembly.
Rakhi was celebrated in history,
One of them was the story of Rani Karnavati,
And king Porus, A Panjabi.
This festival has a great significance,
People throughout the world have proven its
    acceptance.

 Image credit: wallpaperhouse.com

Krishna Janmashtami or Gokulashtami celebrates the birth of Hindu God Lord Krishna who is an incarnation of Lord Vishnu bestowed with the power to destroy all evil.

Krishna Janmashtami

Marks the birth of Krishna,
He was born in jail in Mathura.
Birthed during the star Rohini,
Son of Vasudeva and Devaki,
On his birthday, he was taken on a journey,
To Nandha and his wife Yashoda Devi,
And took to Mathura, their baby,
Kamsa was happily killing the baby,
And then! Appeared the Goddess Lakshmi,
Who told that Krishna was taken to safety.

Kamsa sent hordes of monsters,
But Krishna killed them with his divine powers
Finally, he challenged Kamsa
Killed him and restored the old king Ugrasena.

Vasudeva and Devaki embraced
   Murali and Balarama,
Sent them to study in an Ashrama,
The Duo studied Arts and Dharma,
Fulfilled their Guru Dakshina,
Returned to Mathura with Balarama.

Signifying the onset of the Malayalam calendar month of Chingam, Onam celebrates the appearance of the Vamana avatar of Vishnu and the homecoming of King Mahabali.

Onam

Celebrated in the state of Kerala,
Built on the legend of Vamana,
And Lord Vishnu's incarnation Parashurama.
Onam is a harvest festival,
Respect among various cultures is mutual.
Falls on the 22nd Nakshatra Thiruvonam,
In the Malayalam month Chingam,
Major celebrations take place in Thiruvananthapuram.
An array of boat races,
As well as tiger dances,
Coupled with an onam sadya,
Served royally on the leaf of banana.
People buy and wear new clothes,
Thank the spirits of their ancestors,
By offering them meals.
Celebrated worldwide,
Symbolising Kerala's pride.

Ganesha Chaturthi

Lord Lambodara's re-birth,
On a waxing moon Chaturthi,
Marks the Ganesha Chaturthi.
To keep the terrifying obstacles at bay,
Was given an elephant-head,
For his first head was shed,
When Shiva's anger was misled.

Ganesha's clay idols are made,
In the Pooja room, they are laid,
Huge statues are made of POP,
Dissolved after rituals ASAP.
Shhodashopachara, the 16 rituals are performed,
While Panchamrutham, ghee, and curd are poured,
People sing Bhajans,
While offering Ganesha, Modaks.
The three-bladed druva often considered a weed,
When offered to Ganesha becomes a good deed.
Crown-flower that grows in cemeteries,
As offered to Ganesha who gives good decrees.
Vinayaka swallowed Analasura,
To remove the heat, there was an Archana,
Conducted by 88,000 sages with the druva.

When asked to go three times around the earth,
Moved around his parents' hearth.
He is the first lord,
Who makes the day successful for all.

A resounding cheer
Would be heard all over
Praising Ganesha
And setting the stage for
Grand celebrations.

Image credit: www.freepik.com

Ganesha Chaturthi is a beautiful festival to invoke Lord Ganesh from the divine Kailash Parvat among the mortals on Earth. It is variously known as Ganeshotsav, Vinayaka Chaturthi and Vinayaka Chaviti.

Image credit: Vecteezy

The nine avatars of the Shakti Ma Durga are worshipped through prayers and fasting celebrating the defeat of the mighty Asura Mahishasura by the Goddess.

Navaratri

Navaratri spans nine nights,
Awakening our inner eyes,
It falls between September and October,
So cold, yet we still remember.

Indians celebrate while fasting,
Our legacy is everlasting.
We worship the three forms of Devi,
That is Durga, Lakshmi, and Saraswathi.

Durga killed Mahishasura,
Lakshmi provides wealth,
And Saraswathi gives us knowledge.
All three form the Adi Shakti,
They bless us when we pray with bhakti.

Deepavali comes after 20 days,
To celebrate the arrival of Rama at Ayodhya.
Yes, Gods are honoured in many ways.

After Navaratri, Goddesses statues are
    dissolved in a river,
Yet they will stay in our hearts forever.

Image credit: www.123Freevectors.com

Deepavali signifies the effacing of all evil and lighting up human hearts with hope, joy and prosperity.

Deepavali

Deepavali is the festival of lights,
Where good wins in a fight,
Crackers are plentily burst,
But eating sweets is first.

People celebrate Deepavali from when...
Rama killed Ravana,
And Durga killed Mahishasura.
Statues of Ravana are burnt,
Which states that forces of evil have been turned.

Light is the symbol of victory,
And darkness will be history.

On this day there are no fights,
In enjoyment, we will reach heights.
Houses will be full of light,
People stay awake throughout the night.

Employees have a bonus in their salary,
Gifts and sweets add the merry,
To mark on their memory.

Celebration sets on from a day to five,
Where friends and family are like a hive.

Santa Claus, reindeer, Christmas tree and snowman spread Christmas joy, reminding us of the ultimate sacrifice of Jesus Christ in His attempt to liberate humanity and free them of their sins.

Christmas

Jesus Christ came to this world with a purpose,
To save us from people horrendous,
Angels gave to the shepherds' reports of brights,
Celebrated in December,
For Christ did a lot to remember.

Houses are decorated,
With Christmas lights and are garlanded.
People and families have feasts,
Where each prepares a lot of treats.

Everywhere carols are sung,
In Homes, socks are hung.
Santa Claus brings us gifts,
Comes down through chimneys,
Came after winter festivals,
Started by many German people.

Eggnog is plentily drunk,
Turkeys are made as a hunk.
Who does not love Christmas,
Where crowds move in processions,
To enjoy the holiday seasons!

Culture

Image credit: Vecteezy

Bharatanatyam is a form of traditional Indian classical dance hailing from the temple of Tamil Nadu, enacting stories of Indian mythology.

Bharatanatyam

Tamil Nadu's famous dance form,
Previously called Sadhir Attam,
One of the 8 forms of Indian Nrityam,
Expresses Shaivism, Vaishnavishm and Shaktism,
Part of the epic Silappatikaram,
Several books are written such as Natya Shastram,
Dance of Devadasa clan is Bharatanatyam,
In Bharatanatyam -
Bha stands for Bhavam*,
Ra stands for Ragam*,
Ta stands for Talam*,
And dance is symbolised by the word natyam.
In the 19th century, Bharatanatyam was discouraged,
By the British, it was declined.
But it was later revived,
By all the dancers who strived,
And its standard was raised.
It is now world-famous,
And is adored by masses.

---

* Bhavam - feelings
* Ragam - melody
* Talam - Rhythm

Kathakali transfixes hearts and minds of viewers through the ornamental, magnificent costumes and tells the traditional tale of eternal fight between good and evil.

Kathakali

Classical dance of Kerala,
Top 8 classics in India,
Katha means story,
And Kali means to play.
It is taken from the Natya Shastra,
Started by Sage Bharata.
Similar to the dance Kutiyattam,
Some parts of it are taken from Krishnattam.
Has the most elaborate costumes,
People wear masks that have vividly painted faces,
There are 24 mudras,
And facial expressions called Navarasas.
Expresses a story,
The feelings are captured picturesquely.

Image credit: Flaticon.com

Dedicated to Sun God, this temple in the shape of chariot, showcases exquisite stone carvings and is counted as a world Heritage Site since 1984.

Konark Sun Temple

Located in Konark, Odisha,
Built by King Narasimhadeva,
Dedicated to the Sun God Surya,
Was once called the Black Pagoda,
People gather here for the Chandrabhaga Mela,
Resembles the Sun God's chariot driven by Aruna,
Surya is flanked by Usha and Pratyusha,
His wheels pair each month as Shukla and Krishna,
Shows musicians playing Veena,
Pictures of soldiers are shown in the upana,
Its design manual is found in the Shilpa Shastra,
Sculptures are found on the temple's Shikhara.
Survived through tough times,
Like the Sun, it shines.

Image credit: Vecteezy

Kuchipudi is a classical dance form of Andhra Pradesh, India, that reminds us of poets, temples and spiritual beliefs.

Kuchipudi

Originated in the state of Andhra Pradesh,
An exquisite form of expression.
Dancers wear a cloth, called Agnivastra.
Has many musical instruments,
And lots of ornaments,
Flourished in the Vijayanagar Empire.
Sanskrit scholars like Jayadeva,
Wrote a copy about this dance drama,
Praising its great nritta.
The first prayer is for Lord Ganesha,
After which there is a raga,
Dancers perform while holding a Diya.
During the period of Madras presidency,
The dancers were impacted by poverty.
Now it is spread worldwide,
And everyone in unison admires.

Image credit: Image strokes

Mahabalipuram temple, located in the historic city of the same name, is a UNESCO World Heritage site in Tamil Nadu, symbolizing Indian art, architecture and literature.

Mahabalipuram

A marvellous monument in Tamil Nadu, India
  towards the South East,
Down to the part of the Coromandel coast,
Highlighted in the Bhakti movement,
That took place as a great event,
Mentioned in many foreign testaments,
Has a sculpted head of an elephant,
And a horse in flight,
Especially in Ptolemy's port.
Built by king Narasimha Varman,
Inscribed by the scholar Dandin.
There are many inscriptions,
Describing the victories of Chalukyas,
Has a lot of rathas,
After continuous excavations,
But, the highlight was its Mandapas,
Consists of butterballs,
That stayed intact for centuries,
A powerful wonder,
That stays forever.

Image credit: Favpng

Originating from the temples of Odisha, the classical dance form of Odissi follows the symmetrical body bends with grace and composure.

Odissi

Originated in the Temples of Odisha,
One of the 29 states of India,
Portrays the great Lord Jaganatha,
By a person's splendid abhinaya.
Girls first perform the dances,
Followed by boys, who pretend like girls.
Starts with a Mangalacharana,
Which is a Gods and Goddess's Sloka,
Includes poems like Geetha Govinda,
The dances finally concluded by a play on moksha.
Has three positions,
First the Sambhenga,
Second the Abhenga,
Third the Tribhenga,
And all three are expressed by a Hasta.
Mughals ransacked Pushpagiri,
And destroyed patrons of Odissi like Puri.
During the British colony,
Dancers were reduced to poverty.
A very complex art,
In its development,
Many have played an important part.

Image credit: Pixabay

A brilliant mausoleum, a UNESCO World Heritage Site since 1983, Taj Mahal is a sophisticated example of Indo-Islamic architecture portraying the culture and history of Islamic Mughal rule in India.

Taj Mahal

Taj Mahal or the Rawaza-i-Munawara,
On the southern bank of river Yamuna,
Built-in the splendid city of Agra,
When the Mughals ruled in India,
One of the seven wonders of the World's Tiara.
Dedicated to the memory of his love.
To preserve the identity of his wife,
Whom he was fond of all his life.
Has 4 minarets,
And the detail of motifs,
Took 32 million rupees,
To build it in one of the top cities.
Led by Ustad Ahmad Lahuri,
It houses the King and Queen's sarcophagi,
A great piece of Indo-Islami,
Engraved on it was a lot of calligraphy.
One of the greatest centres,
Keeps up all its honours.

Image credit: Image strokes

Dedicated to Lord Shiva, Tanjore Temple, signifies the ancient Chola dynasty's brilliant feats in the fields of architecture, painting, bronze casting and sculpture.

Tanjore Temple

The temple of Brihadeshwara,
Dedicated to Lord Shiva,
Built by King Raja Raja Chola,
And is popularly called **The temple of Airavatesvara,**
Has the tallest vimana,
Houses a large statue of Lord Shiva's Vahana*,
Lord Nandishwara,
Also India's largest Shiva Linga.
Consists of Shiva's many an Avatara,
Like the Ardhanareeswara,
As well as Harihara.
Has shrines for Lord Ganesha,
And his brother Lord Karthikeya,
Also the river Goddess Ganga.
Built by the Cholas,
Commemorating their victories,
Over the Chalukyas and Pallavas,
And other great kings.
Tamil Nadu's most visited tourist attraction,
Fills everyone with a lot of satisfaction.

---

*Vahana - vehicle

Image credit: freebestmock-up.blogspot.com

Also known by the names of Harmandir Sahib or Darbar Sahib, the Golden Temple gurudwara is the holiest pilgrimage site of Sikhs.

The Golden Temple

Reverently know as Sahib Harmandar,
Reflecting the meaning, abode of God,
Built around a Sarovar,
Made by Guru Arjan from donations of Akbar,
That made him more and more popular,
Later Guru Arjan was killed by Jahangir,
Many such mandirs are there in Patna and Kiratpur,
Highlighted as Sahib Darbar,
To say and share our every prayer.
Sikhs celebrated festivals like Vaishakhi,
And also Diwali,
Bore attacks of rules such as Ahmed Shah Durrani,
Received fresh water from the river Ravi,
It was destroyed during operation blue star,
But was again rebuilt.
A taproot for all Sikhs,
Where a daily feature is langars.

A sprawling sacred site on the banks of River Ganges in Uttar Pradesh, Varanasi is believed to be the abode of Lord Shiva.

Varanasi

Situated in the banks of the Ganges,
Popularly called Benares,
Holiest of all the seven cities,
Honours most of the deities,
Connects Hindus, Jains and Buddhists,
Admired by all the religions,
Here Tulsidas wrote the Ram Charit Manas,
Root of all the Sikhs,
Famous people were born such as
   Kabir and Ravindas,
People who go there get rid of all the Sins,
It's said to have been found by Hindu Trinities,
One of the most important trade centres,
Famous for its muslin, sculpture and perfumes,
A renowned religious centre,
That is built for the better.

Curiosity

Image credit: Wikimedia Commons

The first lady to be elected the General President of the Indian Science Congress, Asima Chatterjee was also the first woman to receive the award of the Doctor of Science by an Indian University in 1944.

Asima Chatterjee

Asima's Childhood interest drawn to botany,
Received a masters followed by a doctoral,
The subject of organic chemistry,
First woman to receive a doctorate,
In the branch of science,
And from the Caltech University,
She had rich research experience.
Discovered anti-epileptic activities,
Her work led to medicinal development,
To combat epilepsy,
Wrote more than 400 papers that were published
    internationally.
Did chemical tests of alkaloids,
And helped in its synthesis,
Appointed as the member of Rajya Shaba,
By the President of India,
She had worked to make lives better,
Google conferred a Doodle in her honour.

Image credit: Public Domain

Chanakya's prominent role in helping the first Mauryan Emperor Chandragupta Maurya to establish the foundation of his empire as his chief advisor goes down the history in golden letters.

Chanakya

An ancient Indian teacher,
And a renowned philosopher.
Identified as Kautilya,
was known as Vishnugupta,
A brahman from Takshashila,
Author of the book Arthashastra.
Served as chief advisor,
To the wealthy Mauryan empire,
Made the ruler as Chandra Gupta,
Also assisted his son Gindusara,
And took revenge in king Dhana Nanda,
Who was the previous king of Pataliputra.
Chanakya was the royal priest,
Who served the Mauryas to a great height,
The Kingmaker,
Bindusara's rescuer,
Under his own hands laid the power.

Image credit: Wikimedia Commons

A leading Indian scientist and politician who is noted for playing a significant role in the development of India's missile and nuclear weapons programs.

Dr. A. P. J. Abdul Kalam

Born to the community, Muslim
In the Hindu pilgrimage site, Rameshwaram
His father was a boat owner and an Imam,
Experienced both Hindu and Muslim Dharam,
Completed education in Schwartz Higher Secondary
   School, Ramanathapuram.
Graduated from Madras Institute of Technology,
Successfully launched the satellite Rohini,
Made the Polar Satellite Launch Vehicle (PSLV),
Which was a great victory.
Served as chief scientific advisor,
To the Indian Prime Minister.
Served as the 11th president of India,
And received the Bharat Ratna.
Was fondly called people's president,
Who unfortunately died of cardiac arrest,
While addressing his beloved students.

Image credit: gplast.com

The Edison of India, G D Naidu, is fondly remembered for the manufacture of the first electric motor in India and initiating the industrial revolution in India.

G.D. Naidu

Popular as India's Einstein,
Was responsible for Coimbatore's wealth creation.
Built India's first electric motor,
He was a genius automobile engineer.
Worked as a waiter,
Later became a transport entrepreneur.
Started the National electric works,
His success made companies,
Along with his inventions,
Made super thin shaving blades,
Distance adjuster for cameras,
And kerosene run fans.
Identified new varieties in cotton, maize and papaya,
Was aided by Sir C.V. Raman and Sir M. Visvesvaraya,
A great educator,
Helping the world was his desire.

Satyendra Nath Bose

Native of Calcutta,
Brought up in the district Nadia.
Attended the Presidency college,
Taught by learned Physicist Jagadish Chandra Bose.
Became a lecturer,
In the physics department of Science College,
  Rajabazar.
Sent this works to Albert Einstein,
On laws of radiation,
Who published them under Bose's
  name in succession.
Invented the Bosons,
The derival was Bose-Einstein Statistics,
Laid the foundations for Quantum Mechanics.
Did some research in Biotechnology,
As well as chemistry, geology and zoology,
And promoted his language Bengali.
Awarded the **Padma Vibhushan**,
Became president of Indian Statistical Institutions,
And a receiver of many felicitations.
Got all the recognitions,
Boosted India's expectations.

A genius of worldwide fame, Sir CV Raman was the first Asian to be awarded the 1930 Nobel Prize in Physics for his discovery of the Raman effect.

Sir C.V. Raman

Born to a family of Tamil Brahmin,
Named Chandrashekhara Venkata Raman,
Finished higher secondary school at
    eleven and thirteen,
Completed honours at 16,
With his student K S Krishnan,
Discovered a new light-based phenomenon,
Received Nobel prize as the first Asian.
On acoustics and optics,
Made many a contribution,
Was motivated by the Mediterranean.
Joined the Indian Financial Services,
Published Bulletin of Indian Associations,
For the cultivation of sciences,
Was presented with the Bharat Ratna,
Smashed it due to Jawaharlal Nehru's
    Scientific law strata.
A highly represented Indian Physicist,
Throughout his life, always was the best and first.

Image credit: Wikimedia Commons

Sir M. Visvesvaraya's contribution in the field of engineering and education leading to constructing dams, reservoirs and hydro-power projects sets the foundation of modern India.

Sir M. Visvesvaraya

The Diwan of Mysore,
Knighted by the British Empire,
Educated from College of Engineering, Pune,
In Designing, Hyderabad's flood protection,
    was Chief Engineer.
Helped build the dam Krishna Raja Sagara,
His birthday is celebrated as World Engineers Day,
In India, Sri Lanka and Tanzania respectively.
Founded the Mysore soap factory,
And the Mysore steel factory in Bhadravati,
Also charted a road construction plan in Tirupati.
Earned the Bharat Ratna,
Was the most popular man in Karnataka,
Visvesvaraya museum was named after him.

Image credit: Wikimedia Commons

Ramanujan's contribution in the field of mathematical analysis, number theory, infinite series and continued fractions established him as a mathematical genius.

Srinivasa Ramanujan

Ramanujan was born in 1887
Made us look at math like heaven.
Had no formal training,
But in math, kept on contributing.

Ramanujan invented ground-breaking theorems,
And made maths follow in perfect rhythms.
Compiled more than 3,900 results,
And wrote various math journals.

A child prodigy by the age of eleven,
Quickly grasped every lesson.

Went to Cambridge,
Despite a lot of hardship.
Everyone found his work amazing,
There was a lot of understanding.

All look at him as a genius,
To the world, he was a big plus.
Shook mathematical foundations,
Overtook his obstacles with patience.

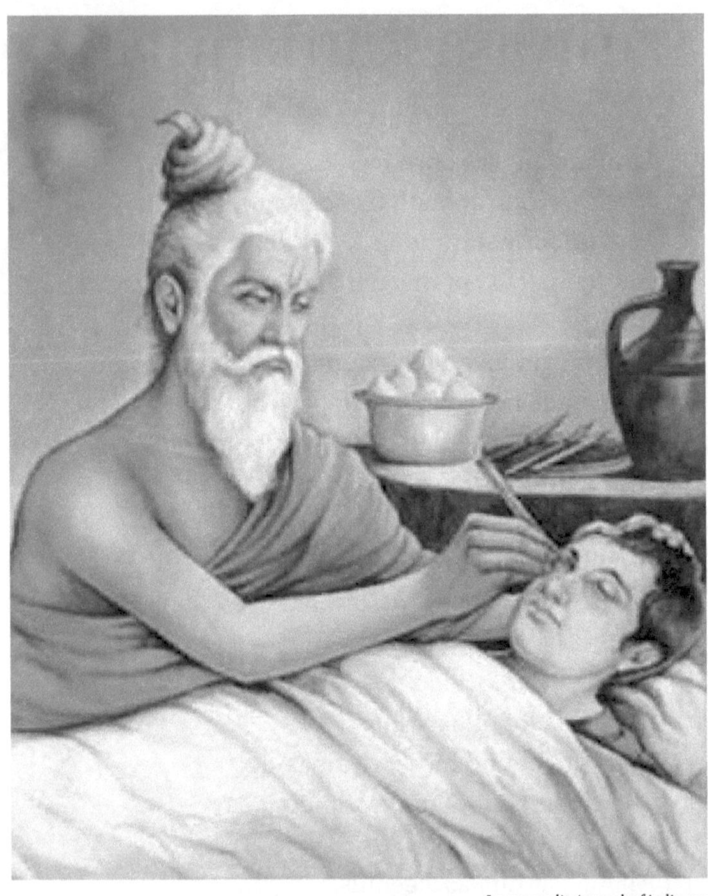

Image credit: journalsof india.org

Titled as the father of Indian surgery, father of plastic surgery and the father of brain surgery, Sushruta was the first to practise rhinoplasty in India.

Sushruta

Best ancient physician,
As well as the first surgeon.
Wrote the Susruta Samhita,
Followed by the Astanga Hridaya,
Laid the foundational text of Ayurveda,
Involved ancient authors called Susruta.
His book contains 1,120 illnesses,
700 medicinal plants,
Preparations from minerals,
And extraction from animal sources,
Susruta's wisdom covers most of the modern
    treatises.
Considered the son of Vishvamitra,
Be the translator Bhishagratha,
In the epic Mahabharata,
He is believed to be residing in the great Himalaya.
Attacked disease and deformity,
By reason and creativity.

Vikram Sarabhai lives in the hearts as a famous Indian physicist, industrialist and astronomer who initiated space research and helped develop nuclear power in India. He won the Padma Bhushan Award in 1966 and the Padma Vibhushan Award (posthumously) in 1972.

Vikram Sarabhai

Hailing from famous Sarabhai family,
Lived his life scientifically,
Founded the Physical Research Laboratory,
Was proficient statistically,
Setup the first market organization in the country.
Led his business in conglomerate,
A man who was very considerate.
Built many institutions,
Like the Ahmedabad Textile Industry Associations.
Awarded the highest civilian
  award Padma Vibhushan,
Helped develop nuclear power,
And India's very own space centre.
A great visionary,
Served his country affectionately.

Courage

Image credit: Wikimedia Commons

Abhimanyu, an incarnation of Varchas, was the son of Arjuna, and a legendary warrior from the ancient Hindu epic Mahabharata.

Abhimanyu

Son of Arjuna and Subhadra,
Was trained by Krishna, Balarama, and Pradyumna,
When Pandavas went on Vanvasa,
And one year of Agnyatavasa,
Upon losing the game of dice with Duryodhana,
Where all their wealth was taken
    along with Indraprastha,
Married princess Uttara,
Daughter of King Virata of Matsya.

An impenetrable armour was given to him,
Along with the bow Rudra,
That made him invincible in Kurukshetra.
Equal to warriors like Drona and Karna,

Aided the Pandavas when Arjuna was
    diverted by Sushrama,
In the Chakravyuha,
Where he was killed by the son of Dushasana,
Then Arjuna swore to kill Jayadratha,
He accomplished that using the Pashupatastra.

After the war,
His son Parikshita
Succeeded the throne of Hasthinapura.

A valiant hero of the early 20th-century Indian independence movement, Bhagat Singh also founded the Naujawan Bharat Sabha and gave up his life revolting against British rule.

Bhagat Singh

Born in Banga, Pakistan,
Was the saviour of Hindustan.
One good radical,
Who believed straight violence was final,
Avenged Lala Lajpat Rai,
By making his killer Scott Squanders die.
Joined Jatin Das in a hunger strike,
Making prison conditions hike.
Was an atheist,
A good Indian socialist.

Members of his family,
Served in Maharaja Ranjit Singh's Army,
His Grandfather followed Dayananda Saraswati,
To influence India's Sanskriti.
A friend of Chandra Shekar Azad,
Because of them, the police became concerned.
Arrested in the Assembly bombing,
British court sent him for executing,
At the age of 23,
Sacrificed himself heroically.

The great founder of Maratha kingdom, Shivaji lives in the hearts of millions for his bravery, warfare tactics and able administration.

Chhatrapati Shivaji Maharaj

Great ruler of Maratha,
Defeated the kind of Golkonda.,
Lived in Shivneri,
And safeguarded his country.

Studied Ramayana and Mahabharata,
Influenced by Krishna and Rama,
Became Aurangazeb's headache,
Who tried to defeat him for a decade,
Kept on evading Aurangazeb's effort,
Shivaji was one great expert.

Was once on a house arrest,
Bringing the guards, escape became perfect,
Finally, the two sides had peace,
And in casualties, there was a decrease,
Lands were given a new lease,
And people exchanged sweets,
Shivaji had grand adventures,
Defeating other enemies a thousand times dangerous.

Image credit: Wikimedia Commons

The third Pandava, demigod Arjuna, is the son of the storm god Indra and a protagonist of Mahabharata symbolising courage, strength, humility, intelligence and wisdom.

Gandivadhari Arjuna

Skilled archer of all time,
Got the Gandiva and became prime.
Was one of the Pandavas,
Rivals with Duryodhana and the Kauravas.
Dronacharya's best disciple,
Overcame all the given obstacles.
Krishna's good friend,
Killed Jayadratha, Karna, and Bhurishriva,
In the Great battle Kurukshetra,
Married Draupadi and Subhadra,
Also lived with Uloopi and Chitrangada,
Was killed by his son Babruvahana,
He was restored to life by Krishna,
Arjuna meditated to Lord Shiva,
To obtain the divine Pashupatastra,
An exclusive figure,
In a mythological scripture.

Lord Kartikeya, the handsome warrior and a yogi, is a symbol of union of polarities and is known for His creative martial abilities to lead an army against Taraka and other demons.

Lord Karthikeya

Incarnated to kill asura, Taraka,
For he could only be killed by Shiva's Putra,
Between them erupted a Yuddha,
Where Shiva assisted him with his Gana,
Taraka threw every Rudra Astra,
Couldn't even touch Karthikeya,
At the end Taraka became his Vahana.
Lord was named Karthikeya,
Because he was raised by the Krithika,
He is mightier than Indra,
So, he became the commander of Devasena.

Possess the mighty weapon, Vela,
Which is his favourite Astra.
With six faces, he became Shanmuga,
The sibling of Lord Ganesha,
The Kanda Shasti Kavasam was dedicated to him,
To appease our every whim.

Image credit: Vecteezy

The widely worshipped Hindu deity, Lord Rama, is considered an embodiment of chivalry and virtue and is the seventh incarnation of Vishnu.

Lord Rama

Son of Dasaratha and Kousalya,
Heir to the gleaming city of Ayodhya,
Sibling of Shatrughna, Bharata and Lakshmana,
Become the consort of Devi Sita,
By breaking the sacred bow Vijaya,
In Swayamvara hosted by King Janaka,
The bane of Lankathipathi Ravana,
Earned an ardent devotee Anjaneya,
Blessed with twin-boys Lava and Kusha,
Lord Vishnu's Avatara.

Was exiled by Kaikeyi,
In his journey, visited sage Valmiki,
He became friends with Vanaras,
Who located Devi Sita after many months.
For reaching Lanka to rescue, Sita,
Nala & Nila built a bridge,
Because of Sugreva's pledge,
Killed all evil,
Gave the world a renewal,
Ruled Ayodhya till the end,
And let Lava Kusha Ascend.

Image credit: Flaticon.com

The sixth avatar of Lord Vishnu, Parashuram, is the revered Guru or teacher of Bhishma, Dronacharya and Karna of Mahabharata and is worshipped for his valour.

Parashuram

Great bhakta of Shiva,
Who taught him every Vidhya,
Killed Kshatriya Kartavirya Arjuna,
Though he was a part of the Brahmin varna,
He cut off a tusk of Lord Ganesha,
While Lord Shiva and Devi Parvati were
    performing Yagna,
There are legends that he created Kerala,
Was a haven for every Brahmana,
After all the violence, retired to do Yoga.

Was the Guru of Drona, Bhishma, and Karna,
Gave them many Ashthras and the bow Vijaya.
Battled with his disciple, Bhishma
To satisfy Amba's plea,
But in the end, the victor was Bhishma.
Rama with the Axe, a blessed Chiranjeevi,
Would live till the end of Kali.

Image credit: Pixabay

The heroic endeavours of Vallabhbhai Patel earned him the sobriquet "The Iron Man of India" and the title of being the patron saint of India's civil servants.

Sardar Vallabhbhai Patel

Iron Man of India,
Who convinced monarchs after millennia,
Was born in Nadiad, Kheda,
And an exceptional diplomat like Krishna.
Became India's Deputy Prime Minister,
Despite every single failure,
Who was actually a successful lawyer.

The great statue of unity,
World's tallest monument structurally,
A tribute from every Gujarati,
Commemorating his saving of India's dignity.

Made discussions with British,
To make their laws abolished.
India's diplomatic pride,
His legacy will always survive.

For uniting all 562 princely states of the Nation,
To build the Republic of India.

Tantia Tope is remembered as the best and the most prominent rebel general who was a kingpin in the Indian Revolt of 1857.

Image credit: Wikimedia Commons

Tantia Tope

General in the Indian rebellion enter
Against the British battalion.
Without any military training,
Territories he started gaining.
Despite being a Brahmana,
Made British powers dampen.
June 1857 he was made Peshwa,
For general havelock feared Sahib Nana.
Aided the Rani of Jhansi,
Took control of Gwalior fort demanding Hindavi
  Swaraji.
The British kept on chasing him,
Tope kept on evading them.
He launched Guerrilla attacks,
To disrupt the British barracks.
Took shelter with the Raja of Narwar,
Who had issues with Gwalior.
British took him to be executed.
He died giving a lot of blood-shed.

Image credit: historyunderyourfeet.wordpress.com

The 18th-century Tamil Palayakarrar and chieftain of Tamil Nadu, Veerapandiya protested valiantly against the British East India Company sovereignty and waged a war against them.

Veerapandiya Kattaboman

An 18th century Tamil Palayakarar,
Was a member of the caste Kambalathar,
Waged a war,
Against the British sarkar.
The Chieftain of Tenkasi,
Who was forced to settle in arid Thirunalveli,
Due to the collapse of Vijayanaga.
Areas around them were occupied by Marvars,
  who took it from the Adivasis,
This was no problem for Tenkasi's residents,
  because they were excellent dry farmers.
Was captured by the British,
Aided by the Pudukottai Rajar,
At age 39 he was hanged in Kayathar.
The Son of the soil,
Lived with prestige, honour and dignity,
And breathed last to reach infinity,
Afterlife speaks of his eternity.
A movie was made of him,
Starring Chevalier Shivaji Ganesan in the film.
A great man,
Historians engraved his lifespan.

Compassion

Image credit: Pixabay

Buddha, the enlightened one, symbolizes an ideal state of intellectual and ethical perfection which can be achieved through following his teachings.

Buddha

Firstly named Siddhartha Gautama,
Who was a part of the clan Shakya,
Of ancient India,
After he saw the suffering of a Purusha,
Meditated and got enlightenment in the Bodh Gaya,
Travelled along the plains of Ganga,
And taught practices such as Jhana,
His teachings were compiled in the Vinaya,
His past lives were portrayed in the Jataka,
And the famous Mahayana Sutra,
Founded Buddhism in the reign of Bimbisara,
The ruler of the Empire of Magadha,
Even a famous Buddhist was Ashoka,
Who spread Buddhism in India,
His son Mahendra,
Was sent to spread Buddhism in Sri Lanka,
He was like Mahavira,
Who was the founder of Jain Tirthankara,
Preached the end of Dukha,
And the emergence of Nirvana,
Considered an Avatara of Narayana,
To uphold the world's Dharma.

Image credit: Clipartstation

Teachers command intense respect from the young and old of the society for their comprehensive role in coaching and mentoring their students and shaping their academic goals and life as a whole.

Dedicated Teachers

One who welcomes to the first day of class,
And teaches us till we pass.
The teacher is our third parent,
Who gives us values abundant.
In teaching, they are dedicated,
Lots of students are educated,
That makes teachers extra motivated.

Teachers are caring,
Make all students outstanding.
Prepare all through the night,
In students, abundant talent they ignite.
Come up with new questions,
To lighten up the lessons,
Carefully curated for all persons,
To carry forward for generations.

Gives us team projects to be active,
Encouraging all students to be collaborative,
Strengthening our ideas to be creative,
Ultimately transforming us to be innovative,
Indeed, we are thankful to you for being super supportive.

Teachers are confident that,
The students they taught,
Will accomplish a lot.

Image credit: www.madrasmusings.com

A living legend, K V Thiruvenkadam, a dazzling scholar and an Indian physician and medical teacher of great repute, has nurtured hundreds of young minds through his expertise and experience.

Padma Shri
Dr. K V Thiruvenkatam

Graduated from Stanley Medical college,
Served people throughout his life's passage.
University of Madras' best outgoing student,
Since then his greatness was evident.
Underwent training in chest diseases,
Had various field expertise,
Conducted trials on tribal medicines,
Mostly including all the ayurvedic preparations,
The late Dr. K. Sanjivi's student,
Founder of voluntary health services,
Gave his pupil good qualities and skills,
Had many endowment orations,
As well as scientific donations.
Recipient of many honours,
Prominent were Padma Shri and Dr. B.C. Roy awards,
Always attracted many hordes.
He was a graduate of a government college,
So with patients, he did less exchange.
Treated people for 2 rupees,
In the spotlight since the movie Mersal's release,
Died in 2019,
His death was completely unseen,
Amidst COVID-19 quarantine.

Image credit: Wikimedia Commons

The 'billion litre idea' of Verghese Kurien, also known as the Father of the White Revolution, started Operation Flood, converting India from an importer of dairy products to India's largest self-sustaining industry creating avenues of rural income.

Dr. Verghese Kurien

Father of the White Revolution,
Fondly called Milkman of India,
Made dairy farming a sustainable occupation.
Invented milk powder,
When the amount of milk was higher.
Linked dairy farmers,
Directly to the consumers.
Worked singularly,
Brought all members of castes to unity,
After independence.
Founded the milk production company Amul,
A person who was always mindful.
Experimented with buffalo milk,
Gave dairy production an extra kick.
His birthday is celebrated as National Milk Day,
And was awarded fifteen degrees honorary.
As a social entrepreneur,
Helped milk production be better,
A light for every dairy farmer.

The second Prime Minister of Independent India, Lal Bahadur Shastri is fondly remembered as "The Man of Peace" for the path of harmony he always followed instead of aggression.

Lal Bahadur Shastri

Second PM of India,
Influenced by the thoughts of Swami Vivekananda,
Born to Sharada Prasad Srivatsa,
Was a follower of Mahatma,
Became an active member of the Indian Congress,
And helped in major Independence movements.
Followed the principle of Satyagraha,
Was sent to jail due to increasing support,
After the Indian Independence,
Became the parliamentary secretary,
Of his home state UP,
And became General Secretary,
Of the All India Congress Committee.
After the death of Nehru ji,
The Prime Minister position was given to Shastri.
Died while signing a peace treaty,
But still lives in all records,
And acts in our accords.

Mohandas Karamchand Gandhi or Mahatma Gandhi is one of the greatest political and spiritual leaders who is aptly addressed as the Father of the Nation.

Mahatma Gandhi

Born in the city-state Porbandar,
In the coastal city Kaithawar,
And his family had the power as Chief Minister.
Studied in Alfred High School,
Where he studied arithmetic and history,
Married Kasturibai at the age of fourteen,
After which he graduated high school at eighteen.
Spent three years in London,
And joined its society vegetarian.
Was a civil rights activist in South Africa,
After which he went back to India.
Fought for India's Independence,
Made policies for nonviolence.
Started Non-Cooperation movement,
And the Quit India Movement,
To remove every British tyrant.
Introduced the proposal Swadesh,
Encouraged Indians to make Khadi.
India attained Independence in 1947,
That made him a popular person.
Unfortunately, he was shot,
And the whole India was distraught.

Mother

A Goddess who gave me this glorious life,
To see the world, gave beautiful eyes.
You make me feel belonged,
And support all along.

True to the saying,
Mata, Pita, Guru, Deivam,
The mother always triumphs,
Teaches us flowery compassion,
In our good deeds, she takes satisfaction.

Mother is my brace when I fall,
Removes my ambiguity.

Bears us for 9 months,
Holds us, till we balance our stands,
Keeps us in heart till her breath,
Soothes through her soul till we breathe.

When we fall, exclaim her name,
She comes running to rescue in the game,
Strives for us to gain fame.
By adhering to the virtuous path.

Blessed are we,
For unconditional love,
Bestowed on us,
From the beloved mother,
To attain eternal bliss.

Image credit: i.pinimg.com

A mother is a selfless, loving individual who sacrifices her wants and needs of her children and works hard to ensure her children grow up as good human beings.

Image credit: Pixabay

The revered Mother Teresa, canonized as Saint Teresa of Calcutta in 2016, is well known as the founder of the Order of the Missionaries of Charity, with the aim to help the poor.

Mother Teresa

Better known as Saint Teresa,
Born in Macedonia,
Served in Ireland then India,
Helped people in Calcutta,
Her biography was written by Navin Chawla,
Spent several months in Patna,
Opened a charity in Tirana,
Again in India,
Developed houses for Leprosy and Malaria,
Helped in religion for treatments,
Hindus received water from the Ganges,
Muslims were read the Quran,
And Catholics received Extreme Unction,
Received awards from President Regan,
And the medal for human service devotion,
At the University of Scranton,
By William J. Bryan.
A renowned Humanitarian,
Received many felicitations.

The great scholar and an independent thinker, Raja Ram Mohan Roy is the revered founder of Brahmo Samaj which is one of the first Indian socio-religious reform movements and is known as one who fought for abolishing the abhorrent practice of Sati.

Raja Ram Mohan Roy

A great Indian reformer,
The title **Raja** was given to him by the second Akbar,
A native of Radhanagar,
Refused all forms of religious prayer,
Was the people's favoured liberator.
Abolished the Sati System,
Fought for his motherland's freedom,
Discouraged all forms of superstitious medium,
And rebelled against his own society's Kulinism*.
Started the Brahmo Samaj,
Rebelled the British for India's swaraj.
Brahmo Samaj believed in one God,
Who resides in all our abode.
Died of Meningitis,
Buried in the Arnole Vale cemeteries.
Films are dedicated to him,
The light lit by him will never dim.

---

*Kulinism - Hindu caste and marriage rules reputedly introduced
by Raja Ballala Sena of Bengal

Image credit: www.thebetterindia.com

The first female teacher of India, Savitri Bai Phule is a great Indian social reformer, educationalist and poet who strove to improve women rights in India.

Savitri Bai Phule

A first female teacher of India,
A Poet from the State Maharashtra,
Born in Naigaon, Satura,
Opened a care centre Balhatya Pratibandhak Griha.
Part of the Mali Community,
Best Female social reformer in history.

Her birthday is celebrated as Balika Din,
To honour every girl as kin.
Was married to Jyotirao Phule,
Who gave her primary education every day.

Established many social trusts,
Provided for all its funds.
She opened a clinic,
To protect people from the Bubonic
   Plague's third pandemic.
While carrying a patient,
She herself became infected.
In order to fight against the disease,
Sacrificed herself with ease.

www.ingramcontent.com/pod-product-compliance
Lightning Source LLC
LaVergne TN
LVHW051442170726
843492LV00002B/506